Carols of Devotion

TREASURES

FROM OUR FAVORITE

CHRISTMAS HYMNS

Doug Samples

Beacon Hill Press of Kansas City
Kansas City, Missouri

Copyright 2003
by Doug Samples

ISBN 083-412-0712

Printed in the
United States of America

Cover Design: Doug Bennett

Library of Congress Cataloging-in-Publication Data
Samples, Doug, 1952-
   Carols of devotion : treasures from our favorite Christmas hymns / Doug Samples.
      p. cm.
   ISBN 0-8341-2071-2 (pbk.)
   1. Carols—History and criticism. 2. Christmas—Prayer-books and devotions—English. I. Title.

   BV530.S26 2003
   242'.335—dc22

                                                        2003014319

10 9 8 7 6 5 4 3 2 1

Contents

Introduction 5

Gloria in Excelsis Deo 7

The Manger of Bethlehem Cradles a King 10

To Follow the Star 12

Far as the Curse Is Found 14

All Is Calm 17

Earthly Things 20

Bless All the Dear Children 23

God Revealed in Us 26

That Beautiful Name 29

The Gloomy Clouds of Night 33

There Is Room in My Heart for Thee 36

Poor, Ornery People 39

The Hopes and Fears of All the Years 42

One Small Light 46

Veiled in Flesh the Godhead See 49

Our Costliest Treasures 52

Life's Crushing Load 56

A Thrill of Hope 61

The Wondrous Gift 65

No Room 68

For unto Us a Child Is Born 71

Wonderful 72

Counselor 75

Mighty God, Everlasting Father 78
Prince of Peace 81
God Is Not Dead! 85
Advent Liturgies 89

Introduction

Christmas is always full of wonderful memories:

- Finding the perfect tree
- The smell of a fresh tangerine
- Sharing bake day with your sisters
- Searching for the most elaborate house decorations
- Eggnog
- Joining a group of friends to go caroling
- Gathering the family to watch *It's a Wonderful Life* and *White Christmas*
- Volunteering to serve at a homeless shelter
- The candlelight Christmas Eve service at church
- Succumbing to sleep on Christmas Eve when you really want to stay up and see Santa Claus
- Waking up to snow on Christmas morning
- Watching your children's faces light up and realizing that you really did surprise them
- Christmas wrapping-paper fights

But maybe the best part of Christmas is singing our favorite Christmas carols. Throughout the season, whether we're in church, the mall, or the car, the days are filled with the songs of Christmas.

In these devotionals we'll look at our favorite carols in ways that we may not have seen them before. With each carol, I have tried to find the crescendo point for that particular song. After reading each carol over and over, I find one key phrase that stands out as the crowning moment and sets the theme for the message behind the song.

After seeing the high point of each carol, you'll find that the message of the song comes alive in tremendous new ways. And there we find wonderful opportunities to consider some of the more significant issues of life.

Some of these devotionals are lighthearted and focused on the joy of celebrating the Christ of Christmas. Others are serious and challenging as we deal with loneliness, materialism, and the lostness of our loved ones.

Hopefully you'll find these pages connecting our hearts as we think together about the concerns of life in the light of these songs of Christmas.

Each devotional closes with a prayer, which is meant not only as the prayerful response of my own heart to the carol but as a suggested prayer for you as well.

Thank you for the wonderful privilege of allowing me to share in your Christmas celebration this year. I hope these devotionals inspire you as they have me.

Gloria in Excelsis Deo

It was an ordinary night on an ordinary hill with a group of ordinary shepherds taking care of their ordinary sheep. And then something *extra*ordinary happened: God showed up! He changed everything that night.

Suddenly a heavenly host of angels appeared (how many angels are in a host?) and scared the daylights out of the shepherds by saying, *Gloria in excelsis Deo*—"Glory to God in the highest and on earth peace, good will to men" (Luke 2:14, KJV).

Their amazing announcement to the stunned shepherds is the most staggering news ever proclaimed on planet Earth: "God himself has come into your world. Today in the city of David, a Savior, a Deliverer, a Redeemer has been born. He has come to bring you grace and peace!"

When was your "today"? When did you hear for the first time that God cared enough about you that He came into your world to knock at your heart's door and offer you His salvation?

Maybe you're like me and heard this news so early in life that it wasn't really earth-shattering news. I don't know about you, but I went to church for nine months before I was even born! I grew up loving Jesus. He has always been a normal and natural part of my life.

Every Christmas season I get to sing these wonderful carols that retell the story of His entrance into our dark, sinful world. My heart, with which I have loved Jesus for so long now, is once again invited to be shocked and surprised by the news that "today He is born! Glory to God! Praise His name!"

Every Christmas season I watch the children's Christmas program at church and marvel at all the new ways we find to tell this old, old story. There's always one child who forgets his or her lines and makes everyone laugh, and one who spends more time waving than singing. And the place they always sing the loudest (and the most off-key) is when they let loose with "Glooooria in egg shell seas Deo."

Every Christmas season there are some who are celebrating Christmas for the very first time as brand-new Christians. I watch them kneel at the altar on Christmas Eve and take Communion as quiet tears of joy slip down their cheeks. And it seems I can hear the angels repeating the good news: "Glory to God in the highest! He is reborn again today!"

So here we are in another Christmas season. Will you give Him permission to be reborn anew and afresh in your heart this Christmas? Will you allow yourself to be surprised by the presence of God during these precious days? Whether you're sitting in church or stuck in traffic, will you keep your heart open to being captured again by the splendor and wonder of the season? How about today? Are you ready for the angels?

You and I are probably as ordinary as the shepherds. That makes us perfect candidates for His appearing. He is excited about surprising us again this Christmas. Hopefully our hearts and eyes are expecting Him. If you look over your shoulder, you may find Him coming up behind you even now to surprise you. Come see! Come adore!

Jesus, sometimes I feel I'm so ordinary and so much a part of You and Your kingdom that I'm beyond the possibility of surprise. You and I have shared a lot of Christmases together. And yet You want to come to me again today. You've been there in all my yesterdays, but You send out Your angels to announce Your coming in the new today. All I can say is "Gloria in excelsis Deo!"

ANGELS WE HAVE HEARD ON HIGH
**Come to Bethlehem, and see
Him whose birth the angels sing;
Come, adore on bended knee
Christ the Lord, the newborn King.
Gloria in excelsis Deo!
Gloria in excelsis Deo!**

The Manger of Bethlehem Cradles a King

Most normal people, when writing something important (like a sermon or a letter to Santa or a Christmas devotional book), want to be locked up someplace quiet by themselves.

With my people-oriented personality and a healthy case of attention deficit disorder, I'm allergic to being by myself. So when I do my writing, I like to be out among people. As I compose, I think about the people around me and how my writing might connect with them. One of my favorite places is a busy bookstore, drinking a hazelnut latte.

But today I'm sitting in the Great Reading Room in the library of the University of Oklahoma. It's an awesome room. As soon as you walk in, it seems that your IQ goes up at least 30 points! The room is 180 feet long and 40 feet wide with a 50-foot-high vaulted ceiling with exposed, intricately carved wooden rafters. Lining the walls are dissertations written by University of Oklahoma doctoral students, including my colleagues Brint Montgomery and Bob Lively.

This room represents power and influence, majesty and might, importance and reputation, academia and learning, entitlement and authority. This is the kind of stately, lavish, impressive, noble place where one would think Jesus should have been born, from which such a king could rule and dominate. It's a fitting location for one who was to be called "Wonderful Counselor, Mighty God, Everlasting Father, Prince of Peace." It's an appropriate place for someone of whom it was said that "the government will be on his shoulders" (Isa. 9:6)

But Jesus was not born in a place of power and influence. His parents were nobodies from Nazareth. Even though He could have clapped His hands and had 10,000 angels at His side ready to do whatever He asked, He chose to live among the most simple and common of people.

Jesus, if You had been born into the upper crust of society, I probably would not have been able to know You. I'm a pretty simple boy from a pretty common family. Sitting in this Great Reading Room makes me feel important, but it's also very intimidating. Thank You for Your willingness to be born in a lowly manger. Your simplicity and humility make it possible for all of us to sing the new song that's in the air.

THERE'S A SONG IN THE AIR
There's a song in the air; There's a star in the sky.
There's a mother's deep prayer
And a baby's low cry.
And the star rains its fire while the beautiful sing,
For the manger of Bethlehem cradles a King!

To Follow the Star

What are your dreams? Do you have any? I'm convinced that too many people have little or no goal or dream in life. They just take whatever life gives them and try to cope the best they can.

At a very early age I accepted Jesus Christ as my personal Savior. As a teenager, I chose to follow a bigger dream by saying yes to the call to full-time professional ministry. I wasn't sure where that call would take me, but I wanted to follow God and dedicate my life to His service.

Following His dream for my life has taken me places I didn't think possible. I've traveled across the United States as a pastor and now as a professor. I'm currently preparing to go on my fourth mission trip to my third continent! I have close, personal friends spread all across the United States and around the world.

Long ago three wise men saw a star that so captured their attention they dropped everything and took the journey of a lifetime.

The end of their search was a dream come true. They found the One who was worthy of their best gifts. They found the One to whom they could ascribe ultimate value and worth. Indeed, they found the long-awaited Messiah. Their dreams led them to the King of Kings and Lord of Lords.

What dreams has God placed in your heart? Are you willing to follow? Will you offer Him the gifts and talents of your life? Will you give yourself away in obedience to follow Him wherever He leads—today, tomorrow, and the next day?

For me it was the words of an old hymn that set His dream ablaze in my heart:

> *I'll go where You want me to go, dear Lord,*
> *Over mountain, or plain, or sea.*
> *I'll say what You want me to say, dear Lord.*
> *I'll be what You want me to be.*

> —Mary Brown

During this Christmas season, let's join the wise men on the journey of a lifetime. Let's dream big dreams for God. Let's embrace His dream and His call. Let's bring Him our very best gifts.

King Jesus, we decided a long time ago to follow Your star, and it's been an adventure-filled journey. We believe that one day we, too, will find ourselves on Your doorstep. We're coming—and we're bringing gifts!

THE FIRST NOEL
And by the light of that same star
Three wise men came from country far;
To seek for a King was their intent,
And to follow the star where'er it went.
Noel, Noel, Noel, Noel!
Born is the King of Israel!

Far as the Curse Is Found

Throughout my pastoral ministry, I've had the marvelous privilege of watching God pour out His blessing of "joy to the world" that goes as far as the curse of sin is found. The best part of being a pastor is seeing lives transformed by the grace of God. It's amazing to watch blessings flow into lives that were once broken by the curse of sin.

I could tell you hundreds of stories of people who have been overwhelmed to discover that even though they thought they were too far gone, God's grace knocked at the doors of their hearts. The Joy of the world has melted the hardness, transformed the darkness, and filled the emptiness of their lives. The curse has been taken away and replaced with blessing.

I've seen this blessing of salvation flow from the heart of the crucified Christ child to overtake
- the curse of alcoholism
- the curse of pornography
- the curse of climbing the ladder of success
- the curse of atheism and agnosticism
- the curse of low self-esteem
- the curse of shame
- the curse of anger with God for the death of a brother or sister

- the curse of anger with God for the death of a father or mother
- the curse of self-sufficiency
- the curse of drug abuse and addiction
- the curse of social anxiety

On and on the stories go. There are so many hideous ways the curse of sin tries to destroy our lives. How I wish I could tell you the names of my friends who fit these stories! How I wish they could tell you their own personal stories of trading in the curse for the blessing!

You probably have loved ones who are far away from God. Some may be so far away from Him that you wonder what it's going to take to get their attention and turn their hearts toward God. Sometimes you've even been afraid they've gone too far.

I have good news for you. During the Christmas season you'll sing this good news again and again. In fact, it's described in one of the carols we sing most often. Every time you hear it, make sure you listen to the best news of all:

> *Joy to the world! the Lord is come. . . .*
> *He comes to make His blessings flow*
> *Far as the curse is found.*
>
> —Isaac Watts

Dear Jesus, You know the friends and family members for whom we pray. We've tried to say the right things, but it never seems to help. We worry about them. Thank You for reminding us that even though they run from You and make their beds in the depths and settle on the far-away side of the sea [Ps. 139], Your presence and blessing can go as far as the curse is found. Thank You for the day Your grace found us, and thank You for the day Your grace will find them! In Your precious name we pray. Amen.

JOY TO THE WORLD
No more let sin and sorrow grow,
Nor thorns infest the ground.
He comes to make His blessings flow
Far as the curse is found.

All Is Calm

Does your family ever fight over the proper way to decorate your Christmas tree? OK—if you don't like the word "fight," would you prefer "argue"? Or maybe "heated discussion" would be more to your liking.

Take your pick of words, but my guess is that all families have different, sometimes even conflicting, ideas about how to decorate the tree. It's because each of us learned the correct way during our growing-up years at home. Problems can arise, however, when the wife's "correct way" doesn't quite match the husband's "correct way."

Let's see if you can identify with any of these differing viewpoints:

- Are you a "real tree" family or a "fake tree" family?
- If you're a "real tree" family, do you drive 25 miles to a tree farm and cut it yourself, or do you get it from the tree lot around the corner?
- Do you flock or not flock?
- Are the lights on the tree all one color or multicolored?
- Does the tree go in the living room or the family room?
- Do you put icicles on the tree or not? (When I

was little, I remember my sister yelling at me for throwing handfuls of icicles on the tree instead of carefully placing them individually on each branch. Granted, her way was a lot prettier, but my way was lots faster!)

- Is your tree decorated in a theme or with a wide assortment of ornaments?
- When do you begin decorating? Are you an early bird who pulls out all the decorations on Thanksgiving weekend, or do you hold out until the week before Christmas?

Of course, the tree is not the only opportunity for family Christmas battles. Do any of the following issues sound familiar?

- How much do you spend on Christmas gifts?
- Do you buy for everyone, or do you draw names?
- Do you open gifts on Christmas Eve or Christmas morning?
- If you're a Christmas morning gift-opening family, are the children allowed to wake Mom and Dad, or do they have to stay in their beds until Mom and Dad are awake?
- Do you open the presents as soon as you get up, or do you eat breakfast first?
- Does your whole family open presents all at once, or do you go one by one?
- Do you pick up all the wrapping paper as soon as each person tears open a gift, or do you

have a big wrapping-paper fight when everyone's done?

- How do you decide which side of the family
  to visit each Christmas? (Isn't that one fun?)
- Do you like a quiet Christmas with just your
  family, or do you prefer having a houseful?

In the middle of a "holly, jolly Christmas," we
can find ourselves a long way from "all is calm."

"You can't possibly be serious!"

"What do you mean sugar cookies instead of
chocolate chip?"

"If you don't help me wrap these presents, someone's going to be staying up and doing it by himself!"

*Jesus, this Christmas we pray for silence in the midst of the
screaming materialism. Give us a calm to replace the storm.
Transform the darkness to bright. Help us embrace each other
with Your tenderness and mildness. Grant our family heavenly
peace throughout this Christmas season. In Your name we
pray. Amen.*

SILENT NIGHT! HOLY NIGHT!
Silent night! holy night!
All is calm, all is bright
Round yon virgin mother and Child!
Holy Infant, so tender and mild,
Sleep in heavenly peace.
Sleep in heavenly peace.

Earthly Things

How many catalogs do you get during the Christmas season? Every day they nearly fill up the mailbox. I think last year we actually got more catalogs than Christmas cards!

Long ago in a century now past, it used to just be the wish book from Sears and J. C. Penney. I would grab the boys and sit on the couch with them and flip through the pages to pick out the gifts they wanted Santa to bring. But now there aren't enough nights to go through the mountains of catalogs that come our way.

There's literally everything from A to Z, and it's all just a toll-free phone call away. The unspoken promise from each catalog is that if I buy some of their products, my life will be better, my children will be happier, and my teeth will be whiter! Money-back guaranteed!

It's a challenge—isn't it?—for us to celebrate Christmas when our society hijacks a *holy day* and turns it into a *holiday*. We're surrounded these days by materialism and marketing. We get caught up in the frenzy of buying gifts for a long list of people and going to a never-ending array of parties.

On top of all this, the shopping malls keep pushing us to start celebrating Christmas earlier and earlier! It used to be the first of December, then right after Thanksgiving. Now we're face-to-face with garland and reindeer in the middle of October!

What are we supposed to do with all this consumer-driven hype? Some people allow it to ruin Christmas for them and everyone around them. They react so negatively to the materialism of our culture that they reject anything that even smells like Christmas cheer.

There's no doubt that all this commercialism can rob us of the true meaning of Christmas. If we're not careful, we can easily be led down the broad road of spending lots of money on earthly things while forgetting that it's supposed to be a time to welcome the heavenly Christ child.

I believe it's possible to enjoy all the festivities of the season without losing our souls to the Grinch. Honestly, I enjoy seeing all the beautifully decorated houses. I'm thankful that some people go to elaborate measures to string lights across their rooftops and through their trees. I look forward to all the parties that give me memorable opportunities to be with family and friends. I even enjoy the shopping and the challenge to find just the right gift for my wife and boys and those I care so much about. I think it's fascinating to walk through the mall and go in and out of stores and hear so many of them playing His songs! I love children's programs at church and bake days.

John Grisham wrote a delightful book titled

Skipping Christmas, which tells the story of Luther and Nora Krank, who decided (it was mostly Luther's decision) to skip Christmas one year. No lights, no tree, no presents, no parties, and no Santa on the roof. None of the trappings of materialism. But in a hilarious ending, Luther discovers Christmas in a marvelous new way. Of course, Christmas has indeed become too commercial, but we don't have to let that steal the joy that comes with the season.

Jesus, every day when we get another catalog, we're tempted by the pull of trying to buy happiness. "Oh, I want that! Oh, I need that! Oh, I have to have that!" Forgive us for what we've done to Your holy day. Help us find a way of enjoying these days in ways that keeps the focus on You. Instead of skipping Christmas, may we truly celebrate these precious days that rush by us so quickly. In your wonderful name we pray. Amen.

AS WITH GLADNESS MEN OF OLD
Holy Jesus, ev'ry day
Keep us in the narrow way;
And, when earthly things are past,
Bring our ransomed souls at last
Where they need no star to guide,
Where no clouds Thy glory hide.

Bless All the Dear Children

Our two boys, Scott and Mark, learned the name of Jesus at a very young age. Soon after Scott was born, we bought a beautiful picture of Jesus holding a small child in His arms. When each boy was an infant, I would hold him in my arms, point to the picture, and softly say, "This is Jesus."

As I rocked my child in my arms, we looked at the picture, and I sang,

> *Jesus loves me! this I know,*
> *For the Bible tells me so.*
> *Little ones to Him belong;*
> *They are weak, but He is strong.*
>
> *Yes, Jesus loves me.*
> *Yes, Jesus loves me.*
> *Yes, Jesus loves me.*
> *The Bible tells me so.*

—Anna B. Warner

As Scott was learning his very first words, I pointed to the picture and asked, "Who is this?"

He would smile and exclaim, "Jesus!"

"And who is Jesus holding?" I would then ask.

"Scott!" he would reply.

"And how much does Jesus love Scott?"

23

Together we would stretch out our arms and say, "This much!"

Two years later, it was Mark's turn for this same beautiful ritual.

"Who is this?"

"Jesus!"

"Who is Jesus holding?"

"Mark!"

"And how much does Jesus love Mark?"

"This much!"

What a joy to watch our children grow up! What a privilege to teach them about Jesus and how much He loves them! What fun it is at Christmastime to let the children help set up the crèche and talk about each of the animals, the shepherds, the angels, the wise men, Mary, Joseph, the manger, and Baby Jesus!

What wonderful memories of all the children's Christmas musicals that Cheryl directed at church! One of the great motivational tools we had with the boys was that "If you do well in the musical, then when we come home you'll each get to open one of your presents." And, of course, they always did well!

In our assorted ornament collection we have "Baby's First Christmas: 1979" for Scott and "Baby's First Christmas: 1981" for Mark. Each year after we put on the very first ornament, which was always that year's new ornament, the boys would get to hang their special ornament in their chosen spot. Now that the boys are grown up, sometimes we have to wait for them to come home to hang their ornaments.

Someday soon we'll give each of them their special ornament to hang on their own tree with their own family. How great! And our collection will be missing years 1979 and 1981. How sad!

It's an incredible privilege to share Christmas with children, to see the awe and wonder in their eyes, to watch them get so excited they can hardly sit still, to read the Christmas story and pass the Good News on to a new generation, to kneel together for prayer as a family.

Precious Jesus, we pray and ask for Your blessings upon our sons and daughters, our grandsons and granddaughters, our nephews and nieces. We entrust them into Your tender care. The greatest prayer of our hearts is that we would all be together forever in heaven with You. In Your incomparable name we pray. Amen.

AWAY IN A MANGER
Be near me, Lord Jesus; I ask Thee to stay
Close by me forever, and love me, I pray.
Bless all the dear children in Thy tender care,
And fit us for heaven, to live with Thee there.

God Revealed in Us

Isn't it surprising to find God in some of the most unusual places? Who would think we could find Him in the feeding trough of a barn in a Podunk town like Bethlehem?

What's even more amazing is the thought of God revealing himself to the world through you and me. He has called us to allow His Spirit to so transform our lives that we take on His holiness and His likeness. He dreams of the day when people look at us and see Him!

In 1 Pet. 2:12 He says it like this: "Live such good lives among the pagans that . . . they may see your good deeds and glorify God."

Wouldn't it be great today if everywhere we went, people looked at us and saw God? By our actions, our words, our kindness, the world could see God because of the way we live.

You and I have the unbelievable privilege of showing God to our world. "We are therefore Christ's ambassadors, as though God were making his appeal through us" (2 Cor. 5:20). Wow!

One of my Internet friends sent me a story that's a great portrayal of what we're talking about. It's about a little boy who wanted to meet God. He knew it was a long trip to where God lived, so he packed his suitcase with Twinkies and a six-pack of root beer and then started his journey.

When he had gone about three blocks, he met an old woman. She was sitting in the park just staring at some pigeons. The boy sat down next to her and opened his suitcase. He was about to take a drink from his root beer when he noticed that the old lady looked hungry, so he offered her a Twinkie. She gratefully accepted it and smiled at him. Her smile was so pretty that the boy wanted to see it again, so he offered her a root beer. Once again she smiled at him. The boy was delighted.

They sat there all afternoon eating and smiling, but they never said a word.

As it grew dark, the boy realized how tired he was and got up to leave, but before he had gone many steps, he turned around, ran back to the old woman, and gave her a hug. She gave him her biggest smile.

When the boy opened the door to his own house a short time later, his mother was surprised by the look of joy on his face. She asked him, "What did you do today that made you so happy?"

He replied, "I had lunch with God." But before his mother could respond, he added, "You know what? She's got the most beautiful smile I've ever seen!"

Meanwhile, the old woman, also radiant with joy, returned to her home.

Her son was stunned by the look of peace on her face and asked, "Mother, what did you do today that made you so happy?"

She replied, "I ate Twinkies in the park with God." But before her son could respond, she added, "You know, he's much younger than I expected!"

Jesus, how many times have we seen You and never recognized You? How often have You sent Your presence to encourage us and cheer us up and we mistook You for the door greeter at church or the janitor at work? Help us to see You! Help us to be like You!

O COME, O COME, EMMANUEL
O come, Desire of Nations; bind
All peoples in one heart and mind.
Bid envy, strife, and quarrels cease;
Fill the whole world with heaven's peace.

That Beautiful Name

Where did your name come from? Do you know for whom you're named? Does your name go way back in family history? Have you ever asked your parents how they came up with your name?

The naming of their children was very significant to the Hebrews, and thus they chose them very carefully. So when it came time for God's Son to come to earth to be born of a virgin, it had to be a very special name. Nothing was left to chance.

The angel of the Lord spoke directly to the virgin's fiancé, Joseph, and said, "[Mary] will give birth to a son, and you are to give him the name Jesus, because he will save his people from their sins" (Matt. 1:21).

Did you know that in the Gospels God's Son is called by that name over 500 times? Throughout the entire New Testament it's found over 900 times.

And if you look through the hymnal, it won't take long to see that the name *Jesus* is one of our favorites also. Can you sing these with me? You take the lead and I'll add the harmony!

All hail the pow'r of Jesus' name!
Let angels prostrate fall.
Bring forth the royal diadem,
And crown Him Lord of all.
—Edward Perronet

Take the name of Jesus with you,
Child of sorrow and of woe.
It will joy and comfort give you;
Take it, then, where'er you go.

Precious name, O how sweet!
Hope of earth and joy of heav'n!
Precious name, O how sweet!
Hope of earth and joy of heav'n!
— Lydia Baxter

There is a name I love to hear;
I love to sing its worth.
It sounds like music in mine ear,
The sweetest name on earth.

O how I love Jesus!
O how I love Jesus!
O how I love Jesus,
Because He first loved me!
— Frederick Whitfield

Jesus is the sweetest name I know,
And He's just the same as His lovely name;
And that's the reason why I love Him so.
O Jesus is the sweetest name I know.
— Lela Long

Just one more. It's not really a Christmas carol, but it could be. It's one of my favorites.

I know of a name,
A beautiful name,
   That angels bro't down to earth;
They whispered it low,
One night long ago,
   To a maiden of lowly birth.

That beautiful name,
That beautiful name
   From sin has pow'r to free us!
That beautiful name,
That wonderful name,
   That matchless name is Jesus!

—Jean Perry

When the time came, God did not just pick a random name out of a hat. His name had been set from the very beginning of time. Even though Jesus was born in obscurity over 2,000 years ago, and even though He died like a criminal at the age of 33, His name is the most well-known name throughout all of history!

When the angel said to Joseph, "You are to give him the name Jesus," he added a qualifying phrase that tells us that the name of Jesus is set apart from all other names: "because he will save his people from their sins."

"Jesus" is an exclusive name. Buddha can't forgive sin. Muhammad can't forgive sin. The Church can't forgive sin. Your parents' religion can't forgive sin.

Only one name can bring forgiveness and salvation —the name "Jesus"!

During this Christmas season, let's cherish the beautiful, wonderful, matchless name of Jesus. He has saved us from our sins. Our hearts are glad. Rejoice! Celebrate! To Him be all glory, honor, and praise!

Jesus, my dear Savior, thank You for the salvation You bring to my life. I would be so lost without You. I want to honor Your exalted, esteemed, and exclusive name. It is at Your name that one day every knee will bow and every tongue will confess that You are Lord and Savior of all humanity. I choose to bow and confess that here and now today! Merry Christmas, Jesus!

THAT BEAUTIFUL NAME
That beautiful name,
That beautiful name
From sin has pow'r to free us!
That beautiful name,
That wonderful name,
That matchless name is Jesus!

The Gloomy Clouds of Night

Some of the loneliest times of my life were Friday nights on my Christian college campus when everyone had a date except me and five or six other guys.

On a campus of 2,000 students, I felt alone and forgotten. I especially remember my junior year when I looked out my window and saw all the people. Everybody had somebody—except me!

Over the years I've made a couple of discoveries about loneliness. I've learned that it's not a dragon I can slay once and for all, putting it forever in my past. I've also learned that I'm not the only one who fights this battle. Many of us know what it's like to carry around burdens that weigh us down and seem to separate us from those around us. We say to ourselves, *It's too sensitive to talk about. No one would really understand, so I'll just keep it to myself.*

In these difficult days we can feel all alone with a problem that gnaws away at us, taking painful bites out of our joy, sapping our strength and beating us into submission until we feel like screaming.

Scattered throughout the Bible we find individuals dealing with feelings of loneliness that can sound very familiar to us. We have everything from

Martha feeling alone because Mary is not pulling her weight (Luke 10:40) to Elijah curled up all alone under the broom tree crying out, "I have had enough, LORD. . . . Take my life" (1 Kings 19:4).

And then there's Paul in the fourth chapter of 2 Timothy. At the end of his life we hear his lonely lament: "Demas . . . has deserted me" (v. 10), "Alexander . . . did me a great deal of harm" (v. 14), and "at my first defense, no one came to my support, but everyone deserted me" (v. 16).

To Martha, Elijah, Paul, and all who battle depression and loneliness come these precious words:

> O come, Thou Dayspring, come and cheer
> Our spirits by Thine advent here.
> Disperse the gloomy clouds of night,
> And death's dark shadows put to flight.
>
> —Latin hymn

In Martha's distress, Jesus wants to say, "Relax. It's all right. I'm here!" With Elijah, the Spirit of God comes in the gentle whisper of the wind to give him new peace and purpose. And in the midst of painful loneliness, we can still hear Paul proclaim, "Even when I felt alone, the Lord was with me. He never left my side. He was my strength."

Into the midst of our struggles, failures, disappointments, and loneliness comes the Creator God of the universe in the very flesh of His Son, Jesus! His cheer brightens the darkest night. His joy overcomes the deepest sorrow. His peace calms the fiercest storm. His forgiveness erases the ugliest sin. His power heals the broken heart.

Into our loneliness God wants to come and dwell among us. He wants to "pitch His tent" in our camp! Can you believe it? He chooses to live in our neighborhoods, our houses, our hearts.

When we need a friend, He wants to be there. When others disappoint us, He wants to be there. When it seems as though nobody understands what we're going through, He wants to be there. When we've lost our dearest loved one and have to spend Christmas alone, He wants to be there. When we're feeling very single in a couple's world, He wants to be there. When we're all by ourselves in the dorm on Friday night, He wants to be there.

Dearest Jesus, how can we ever adequately thank You for the joy You bring to our lives? Into the darkest, gloomiest times of our lives, You bring the Dayspring of Your presence to brighten our world! Maybe the dark and lonely times of our lives are meant to help us realize how much Israel longed for Your coming so long ago. The days we spend in the shadows make us aware of how much we long for Your coming. O come, O come, Emmanuel—be with us!

O COME, O COME, EMMANUEL
O come, Thou Dayspring, come and cheer
Our spirits by Thine advent here.
Disperse the gloomy clouds of night,
And death's dark shadows put to flight.

There Is Room in My Heart for Thee

When Cheryl and I go to our favorite Mexican restaurant, we almost always order the same thing —our favorite Mexican dish, fajitas. You may know what fajitas are, but do you know what farolitas are?

As you drive through town during the Christmas season and look at all the lights, have you seen any homes decorated with those small paper lunch bags with candles in them? They're usually lined up in rows along driveways and sidewalks to create a lovely entrance to the home.

They're called "farolitas" (also known as "luminarias") and trace their origin all the way back to 18th-century Spain, where small bonfires were used to light the way to the Christmas Eve mass. Today farolitas light the path to show that "this home has room for the Christ child. He is welcome here."

In the rural Southwest of the United States, with its wonderful Spanish-Mexican influence, farolitas are an important part in the celebration called "Las Posadas," which reenacts Mary and Joseph's search for a place to rest before the birth of Jesus. Families often gather in a friend's home, and the children, pretending to be Mary and Joseph, go from room to room asking to be allowed in. But each time they're turned away: "Go away! We're too busy! Find someplace else!" Finally, when they come to the designated room, they're welcomed inside, and Baby Jesus is carefully nestled into His cradle.

The Christmas season is undoubtedly the busiest time of the year for most people. So many parties to attend, gifts to purchase, decorations to put up, cookies to bake, cards to mail, and miles to drive.

On top of all the normal, ongoing responsibilities of life, we all have extra "to do" items to add to our lists. All the stores scream at us to come and check out their "biggest sale ever." Every catalog known to humanity finds its way to our mailboxes. Our places of employment generate additional work for us to do in order to close out the year. Even the church schedules a multitude of special events (including children's play practice and Sunday School class parties) as a way of helping us celebrate the season. (When I was a pastor, one Christmas season my wife and I had five parties to go to in one evening!) And then there are all the Christmas specials on television that we have to watch, as well as seeing *It's a Wonderful Life* at least three times.

I wonder how you even find a few quiet moments each day to read these Christmas devotionals.

Somewhere in the midst of all this Christmas chaos, we're supposed to stop and reflect on the unbelievable gift of Christ's coming into our world. There are some years when we don't even get our Christmas cards sent out until Valentine's Day! Don't you wish that God could have scheduled Christmas at a quieter time of the year?

What a perfect time to remind ourselves of the priority that Christ holds in our life! During these wonderful days of celebrating, let's not let the busyness crowd out the Savior. Let's put out the welcome mat and let Christ know that we look forward to His coming.

See if you can find a house this Christmas season that's decorated with farolitas. I saw one just today as I was coming home from work.

"O come to my heart, Lord Jesus; / There is room in my heart for Thee." Forgive me for all the times when my life is as full and overcrowded as the Bethlehem inns were on that first Christmas night. I want the Christmas lights in our home and the farolitas along our driveway and sidewalk to let You know that You're welcome here.

THOU DIDST LEAVE THY THRONE
The foxes found rest, and birds their nest
In the shade of the forest tree;
But Thy couch was the sod, O Thou Son of God,
In the deserts of Galilee.
O come to my heart, Lord Jesus;
There is room in my heart for Thee.

Poor, Ornery People

Every Christmas season, Cheryl and I think back to our first Christmas in sunny California. Around 10 P.M. on Christmas Eve that year, we received a phone call from a middle-aged lady who had recently started attending our church with her husband. They were a jet-set couple: tanned, attractive, financially well off, superconfident, and enjoying life in the fast lane. This was the fourth marriage for both of them.

The voice on the other end of our Christmas Eve phone call was tearful and desperate. She was drunk; he was drunk. They had gotten into one of their many arguments, and he had started beating her. "Can you come and help me?" she pleaded. "I know it's Christmas Eve, but I don't know what to do."

Cheryl and I took off our Santa hats and put on our pastor hats. We rousted our children from their beds, hurriedly dressed them, and drove them to our adopted California grandma's house. When we got to the couple's house, we found that he had taken off for another round of drinks. While Cheryl stayed home with the wife, I tracked down the husband at his favorite bar.

I never realized how ugly a bar full of drunks could be on Christmas Eve. It was like nothing I had ever experienced before. While my life experience had been wrapping presents in front of the fire, there was another world out there that was cold and hard.

I tried to get my friend to calm down, and we finally left the bar for Denny's to get some coffee. Sometime after 1 A.M., he was finally ready to talk with his wife, so I called Cheryl and had her and the wife meet us at Denny's. As soon as they walked in the door, the husband and wife started screaming at each other. The wife turned and ran out the door, with Cheryl chasing after her.

Eventually I managed to get the husband back home, but Cheryl and the wife weren't there. They finally arrived at 2:30 A.M., and we encouraged them to declare a truce for the rest of the night and through Christmas Day.

Cheryl and I left, picked up the boys at 4 A.M., went home, and collapsed in bed—only to be awakened two hours later by Scott and Mark jumping on us in bed and yelling, "Santa was here! Santa was here!"

I wish I could tell you that this Christmas Eve rescue mission ended with our friends receiving and experiencing the new life of Christ. Honestly, I'm sorry to say that they eventually drifted away from our church, and we lost contact with them.

I think about that couple every Christmas, especially on Christmas Eve. I wonder whatever happened to them. I wonder if they ever found peace in their hearts. I wonder if their marriage survived the stresses of life. I wonder why Jesus died for ornery people like them. And I wonder why Jesus died for ornery people like me!

Jesus, sometimes I wonder why You love me so much. I certainly don't deserve it. It's hard for me to realize that You have so much love that You can afford to lavish Your love on millions of people like me who respond to your call and still have unending love to pour out onto the millions of people who never respond to Your invitation at all. Your love is overwhelming!

THOU DIDST LEAVE THY THRONE
Thou can'st, O Lord,
with the living word
That should set Thy people free;
But with mocking scorn,
and with crown of thorn,
They bore Thee to Calvary.

The Hopes and Fears of All the Years

"The hopes and fears of all the years are met in Thee tonight." How can that be? How can Jesus gather up all the hopes and fears of all the years? That seems like a tall order.

This beautiful truth can be seen clearly in the lives of two characters in the Christmas story: Simeon and Herod. These two individuals have radically different reactions to Jesus. To Simeon, Jesus personifies the greatest hope of his life. But for Herod, Jesus strikes fear and terror in his heart. You and I will most likely have one of these same two responses to the Christ child.

Luke 2:25 tells how Simeon spent every day in the Temple waiting for the consolation, or fulfillment, of Israel. He watched for the Messiah, whom the prophets of old had told about.

It has been suggested that Simeon embodies and represents the Old Testament. His hopes were the hopes of the Old Testament. His yearning was the yearning of all of Israel. His desire was to see the One promised long ago.

When Mary and Joseph arrived at the Temple with Baby Jesus, Simeon knew who the Child was.

Somehow he knew this was the One for whom he had been waiting so long. Simeon's heart leaped, his tears flowed, and his old crippled arms reached out to greet this new Hope.

As Simeon wrapped his arms around the Christ child, it was as if Jesus were being embraced and welcomed by all of the Old Testament. As we listen to the solitary voice of Simeon, we can also hear all the collective voices of the Old Testament crying out these words of welcome: "Sovereign Lord, as you have promised, you now dismiss your servant in peace. For my eyes have seen your salvation, which you have prepared in the sight of all people, a light for revelation to the Gentiles and for glory to your people Israel" (Luke 2:29-32).

Just like Simeon, all of the Old Testament was designed to hope for the Messiah. As he rejoiced, he also acknowledged that he could now depart in peace. In no way does this mean that the Old Testament is no longer valuable or worthwhile. On the contrary, the coming of Jesus validates every page and every story. The New Testament has brought peace (shalom, wholeness, completeness) to the Old Testament. The old message is more alive now than ever before. The long-awaited hope has now become real and alive. The vagabond, illusive, transient hope has finally found a home in Jesus!

Just as Jesus symbolized hope for Simeon, He was the fear of all fears for Herod. When Herod first caught wind of Jesus (Matt. 2:1-3), he knew immediately that this coming sounded trouble for his kingdom. Instead of responding with praise and worship, like Simeon, he reacted with fear and retaliation—"There's room in this town for only one power, and I'm it! Any power that challenges me will face my wrath."

Herod represents all the kingdoms of the world that clamor for authority and priority in our lives. And he was perceptive enough to realize that there's room for only one on the throne. As a result, Jesus should bring fear to all other competing authorities. To embrace Him as Lord means the release of all contenders for first place in our lives.

If we're to be serious in our celebration of the Christ of Christmas, we need to be aware, like Herod, that He has come to declare war on all other kingdoms. His coming brings not only hope for the fulfillment of all God's promises but also fear and death to all God's rivals.

Jesus, as Savior, You bring hope to our world. We wander back and forth trying to find the Promised Land, seeming to spend more time in the wilderness. But when we find You (or rather, when You find us) our hearts leap for joy as we realize the fulfillment of all we've hoped for. As Lord, You also bring fear to the world. You've come to rule on the throne of our lives and will not share that throne with Herod. Today we renounce other loyalties and invite You to rule and reign over our lives.

44

O LITTLE TOWN OF BETHLEHEM

O little town of Bethlehem,
How still we see thee lie!
Above thy deep and dreamless sleep
The silent stars go by.
Yet in thy dark streets shineth
The everlasting Light;
The hopes and fears of all the years
Are met in thee tonight.

One Small Light

In the opening words of John's Gospel we read these words: "In him [Jesus] was life, and that life was the light of men" (v. 4). At Christmas, we celebrate the coming of light into a world of darkness. It's that light that makes the difference in the world.

In Christ, mankind finds the answer to his problems, the satisfaction of his desires, the enjoyment of his dreams, the fulfillment of his appetites, the harmony of his soul.

No matter who we are or what we do, Jesus is the ideal of ideals!

To the astronomer, He is the Bright and Morning Star
To the artist, He is the One Altogether Lovely.
To the baker, He is the Living Bread.
To the builder, He is the Sure Foundation.
To the doctor, He is the Great Physician.
To the engineer, He is the New and Living Way.
To the farmer, He is the Sower and Lord of the Harvest.
To the geologist, He is the Rock of Ages.
To the jeweler, He is the Pearl of Great Price.
To the juror, He is the Faithful and True Witness.
To the lawyer, He is the Counselor and Advocate.
To the musician, He is the True Harmony.
To the philanthropist, He is the Unspeakable Gift.
To the philosopher, He is the Wisdom of God.
To the preacher, He is the Word of God.

To the sculptor, He is the Living Stone.

To the student, He is the Incarnate Truth.

To the theologian, He is the Author and Finisher of our Faith.

To the traveler, He is the Way.

To the sinner, He is the Savior.

To the Christian, He is the Guide and Stay.

He is the Lover of the Poor, the Healer of the Sick, the Matchless Teacher, the Incomparable Philosopher, the Ideal of Ideals and the King of Kings (Russell V. DeLong, *The Unique Galilean* [Kansas City: Beacon Hill Press of Kansas City, 1966], 12-15).

God has given us the great gift of Jesus in hopes that we will receive Him for ourselves and pass Him on to others. God has lavished us with His love and grace, not just to transform our darkness into light but also so that we will share our light around the world and around the corner.

But you may say, "I'm not that big. I'm nobody special. I'm not very important. I don't have a lot of influence. What difference could I make?"

The next time a lightbulb burns out at your house, I would love to hear you say, "Oh, it's only one light. We have other lightbulbs in the house that are still burning. I don't really need that light next to my bed. I think I'll just go without it."

It's amazing how one small light that's missing gets a lot of attention. At our house we can't even go one night without the tiny little nightlight out in the hallway.

"But it's only one light—no one will miss it."

"It's only one life—no one will care."

"He's only one child—no one will ever remember Him."

Jesus not only wants to be the light of our lives but also calls us to "let [our] light shine before men, that they may see [our] good deeds and praise [our] Father in heaven" (Matt. 5:16).

Dear Jesus, thank You that what started out as one small light became the Light of the World. Your kingdom of light has won the victory over the kingdom of darkness. Your light has transformed my life. Thank You so much for that gift—the best gift of all time! Help me pass this Light on to my family and friends.

ONE SMALL CHILD
One small child in a land of a thousand
One small dream of a Savior tonight
One small hand reaching out to the starlight
One small city of life.

One small light from the flame of a candle
One small light from a city of might
One small light from the stars in the endless night
One small light from a face.*

*One Small Child," by David Meece. © 1971 Word Music, Inc. All rights reserved. Used by permission.

Veiled in Flesh the Godhead See

What are the most beautiful sights you've ever seen?

Here are my top five:

No. 5. It's a tie between the view after you come through the tunnel and see the entire Yosemite Valley and the view of Yosemite Valley from the top of Half Dome.

No. 4. It's a tie between an early-morning sunrise over the Atlantic or a flaming sunset over the Pacific.

No. 3. The sight of a full, open parachute during the one and only skydiving experience of my life.

No. 2. It's a tie between the birth of each of my two wonderful boys.

No. 1. The stunning beauty of my bride in her wedding dress on the day she became my wife.

How do I describe something so indescribable? How do I explain to someone how beautiful something is? How do I help people see it the way I see it? Writers use words, artists use colors, musicians use notes, sculptors use stone or clay.

When God took His shot at describing the indescribable, He used flesh! John 1:14 says, "The Word became flesh and made his dwelling among us." This is a verse that we Christians hear often. Sometimes we read it so casually and nonchalantly that we lose track of how unbelievably radical and revolutionary it really is. But John knew that the indescribable had happened, and he found the right words to describe it.

The eternal, preexistent, infinite, unfathomable Logos *became flesh*. He didn't just clothe himself with flesh like the "invisible man" putting on a coat and hat so we could see Him. He *became* flesh.

John does not say that Jesus became a man—he says He became *flesh* (*sarx* in the Greek). He does not say Jesus became a Jew—he says He became *flesh*. He does not say Jesus became white or black or olive-skinned—he says He became *flesh*. Jesus became that which all of us have in common: *sarx* —flesh! He was not part human or half human—He was *totally* human.

John can't fully explain it, but he knows what he saw. "Folks, we actually saw Him. We touched Him. We ate with Him. We walked with Him. We sailed on the Sea of Galilee with Him. We laughed together, cried together, prayed together. And when we saw Him, we were beholding the glory of God himself!"

In Christ, God became approachable, accessible, visible, recognizable, touchable, relevant, and vulnerable. If God had forever remained in His aloneness, we would have no choice but to remain in ours. We do not have the power to initiate a relationship with Him. But in Christ, God has chosen to become known and has opened the door and invited us into relationship with Him.

It's in this encounter that we find meaning, fulfillment, forgiveness, salvation, redemption, cleansing, purpose, and calling.

Jesus, it's really hard to explain the Incarnation. John obviously did a lot better than I did. I can't even explain how awesome it is to jump out of an airplane and then look up and see my parachute open and realize that today is not the day I'm going to die! Thank You for bringing the glory and splendor of God into our world. Thank You for making Your home here among us. You had to be with us so that we could be with You. Thank You.

HARK! THE HERALD ANGELS SING
Christ, by highest heav'n adored!
Christ, the everlasting Lord!
Long desired, behold Him come—
Offspring of the Virgin's womb.
Veiled in flesh the Godhead see;
Hail th'incarnate Deity,
Pleased as man with men to dwell,
Jesus, our Immanuel!
Hark! the herald angels sing,
"Glory to the newborn King."

Our Costliest Treasures

One of my favorite Christmas traditions is searching for the perfect dated ornament for our tree. Sometimes we find the right one on our very first try. Other times we end up looking through dozens of stores in several states to find the perfect one. One year I found our ornament on a mission trip to Brazil. Another year, Cheryl had to pick out one by herself because we had waited until the last minute, and I couldn't get free to go with her.

Every year as we prepare to decorate the tree, we carefully lay out the dated ornaments that we have chosen for each year of our married life. One of the most interesting observations is to see reflected in the ornaments the years when we had the least amount of money. Like the second year of graduate school when Cheryl changed jobs and took a 50 percent pay cut in order to get a 50 percent fulfillment raise. Or the early years of paying off school loans and starting our family while pastoring a small home mission church.

All the ups and downs of our financial life are reflected in the annual display of our collection of dated ornaments. Another reminder is the lava lamp that we bought as the only gift we could afford for our first Christmas together—$14.99 for that beauty. We've kept it so long that it's now back in style.

That first Christmas we could afford to budget only $25 for all our Christmas spending. We bought two boxes of red ornaments (which we still have) for 88 cents each, one string of lights, a small real tree, and the lava lamp.

That left about $7 for gifts for our family members. And so with our neighbors and equally impoverished fellow grad school friends, Lamar and Vickie Brantley and Thom and Theresa Havener, we went to an arts and crafts store for three Tuesday nights and hand painted ceramic plaques for both sides of the family. They weren't all that attractive, and surely not very expensive, but they represented our deep love for our cherished family.

Cheryl and I often look back at that first Christmas together, our poorest Christmas, as our best Christmas of all. It is by far the most memorable.

You and your family undoubtedly have as much fun as we do trying to find the perfect gift for everyone on your Christmas list. You always want to find something as inexpensive as possible that will still reflect the deep love you have for your family and friends. And many times it's the simplest gifts that signify the greatest love.

In my Christmas file is an unidentified story that I have adapted here:

> When our son Pete was six, it was a depression year and the bare essentials were all we could afford.

With Christmas a week off, we told Pete that there could not be any store-bought presents this year. "But we can make pictures of the presents we'd like to give each other."

For the next few days each of us worked secretly, with smirks and giggles. And on Christmas morning, our tiny living room was filled with gifts! Of course, they were only pictures of gifts, to be sure, cut out or drawn and colored and painted. But they were presents, luxurious beyond our dreams: A slinky black limousine and a red motorboat for Daddy. A diamond bracelet and a fur coat for me. Pete's presents were the most expensive toys cut from advertisements.

Daddy's best present to me was a watercolor he had painted of our dream house. My best present for Daddy was a sheaf of verses I had written over the years, verses of devotion and of sad things and amusing things we had gone through together.

Naturally we didn't expect any "best present" from Pete. But with squeals of delight, he gave us a crayon drawing of flashy colors and the most modernistic technique. But it was unmistakably the picture of three people laughing—a man, a woman, and a little boy. They had their arms around one another and were, in a sense, one person. Under the picture he had printed just one word: US. For many years we have looked back at the day as the richest, most satisfying Christmas we ever had.

When we go searching for "our costliest treasure" to offer our King, remember that the best gift of all may be the most simple: ourselves.

Jesus, since we have to be careful not to overspend at Christmas, we're always looking for a good bargain: something that looks good and makes a good impression on our friends and family and also lets them know that we love and care about them. But we don't want to look on the bargain table to find a gift for You. We don't want to just look good— we want to be good! There's only one way for that to happen, and that's to give You the gift of US.

AS WITH GLADNESS MEN OF OLD
As they offered gifts most rare
At that dwelling rude and bare,
So may we with holy joy,
Pure, and free from sin's alloy,
All our costliest treasures bring,
Christ, to Thee, our heav'nly King.

Life's Crushing Load

I really love life! Especially at Christmas. I love to love God and enjoy Him completely. Most days, year round, I wake up happy and blessed, expecting to have a great day. One of my favorite lines is "You either get happy or fake it!" My dad taught me that positive attitude a long time ago, and I've passed it on to my boys. It saves a lot of family arguments.

But I imagine there have been times for you—as there have been for me—when life is just too painful to get happy or even fake it. I'm not talking about the normal difficulties of day-to-day living. Most of us realize that those are just speed bumps on the road of life and that we have to slow down and get over them. We can even deal with getting hit with two or three major challenges at once.

The rub comes when we have four or five or six or eight issues crashing in on us all at one time. It's like a chain-reaction car wreck on a foggy freeway —problems pile into each other, and you're caught somewhere in the middle. Helpless. Numb. Dazed. How did I get here? How do I get out? Which way is up?

You know what I'm talking about, don't you? You've faced those crushing days. What's your limit? How many issues can you deal with and still maintain your emotional and spiritual balance? How much of a load can you carry and still choose to get happy or fake it?

My limit is somewhere around 18. As I said, I'm a pretty optimistic, fun-loving guy, and it takes a few bangs over the head to get me down. But one afternoon I found myself in tears draped over the altar of our church. I was weary of life, worn out emotionally, spiritually, and physically.

I remember asking myself, *What's the problem here? Snap out of this and get back to enjoying life!* But I couldn't. I was trapped in a fog bank with screeching, crashing cars spinning all around me.

I finally went to my office and got a pad of paper, came back to the altar, and started writing. About an hour later I had managed to list 18 different issues tearing at me from inside: Personal health concerns, painful family issues, difficult situations at church.

I was living under the deepest fog of "unjoy" I had ever faced. Every day on my early morning walk, I tried to pray. My path took me past one of the many aqueducts that run through the Central Valley of California. And every morning the "demons in the ditch" (after a while, we were on a first-name basis) would greet me with *Hey, Doug, why don't you jump in? You could float awhile, and then you could sink, and it would all be over!*

And every morning I would say to them, *No— not this morning. Maybe tomorrow. I think I'm going to try to*

57

ride this day out! Later, as I ran back to the house and passed the aqueduct again, I could hear them say, *See you tomorrow!*

Sure enough, the next day, there they were with the same invitation. And again I would say, *No—not this morning. Maybe tomorrow. I think I'm going to try to ride this day out!*

That conversation went on every morning for several months between me and the "demons in the ditch." For me it was what some people call "the dark night of the soul." Although I went about all my pastoral duties of smiling and caring, preaching and teaching, leading and planning, every morning I faced hand-to-hand combat with the forces of evil.

I wish I could tell you of one miraculous morning when I was delivered from that dark, spiritual fog, but I don't remember anything like that happening. What I remember most about those days is that I did not face them alone. God himself was with me on each and every one of those early morning walks.

Even when I didn't have deliverance, I had a Deliverer! Even when I couldn't find redemption, I had a Redeemer! Even when "life's crushing load" had me so beaten down that I could hardly keep my balance, there was One who held me safe and secure in His mighty hand. If you had looked behind me on those early morning walks, you undoubtedly would have seen only one set of "footprints."

I know this is the Christmas season, and I know these devotionals are supposed to reflect the joy and good cheer that come with Christmas. However, I could not get past the challenging, comforting words of this beautiful carol. It's one that reminds us that in the middle of "midnight," a Savior has been born.

I also know that the Christmas season can be an emotionally difficult time for many people. Hidden beneath the canopy of fa-la-la-la-la is the reality that the normal struggles of life are often intensified during the holidays. In the midst of all the laughter and celebration of the season, some of you will struggle with "life's crushing load" during these days.

I can't promise you deliverance—but I can promise a Deliverer! I can't promise redemption—but I can promise a Redeemer, whose name is Emmanuel, God with us! Jesus the Christ wants to put His strong, loving arms around you and say, "*O rest beside the weary road / And hear the angels sing.*"

They're singing for you today. Right in the very midst of your weariness, let Christ be your rest today. Rest in Him. Walk this day in His arms!

Dear Jesus, most days are wonderful, but some days are not. Most days we feel blessed, but some days we don't. Most days we rejoice to hear Your voice, but some days the "demons in the ditch" almost drown You out! For those "some days" You offer rest to our weary, foggy souls. Thank You!

IT CAME UPON THE MIDNIGHT CLEAR

And ye, beneath life's crushing load,
Whose forms are bending low,
Who toil along the climbing way
With painful step and slow,
Look up! for glad and golden hours
Come swiftly on the wing.
O rest beside the weary road
And hear the angels sing.

A Thrill of Hope

I don't like to wait. Do you? In our fast-paced world, it's hard to wait for anything.

In the early days of settling the plains of America, if you missed the stagecoach going west, you didn't worry about it. You just caught the next one —next month! These days we get all irate if the fellow in front of us is slow and causes us to miss a stoplight!

Before the days of remote controls for our television sets, we used to sit calmly on the couch and enjoy the commercials. Today we flip channels so fast that we can watch three different movies (or ball games or news shows) at once and never see a single commercial.

Long ago, in a world that's hard for most of us to imagine, the world waited for 400 years. The Old Testament prophets had promised a Messiah. A Deliverer. A Savior. But nothing happened. For 400 years nothing happened. The people waited, but God was silent.

Every once in a while a significant leader came along, and everybody got excited. "Maybe *this* is the Messiah we've been promised!" But again and again they were disappointed.

Then finally, "When the time had fully come, God sent his Son" (Gal. 4:4).

What was so special about that particular time in history? Why was God silent for 400 years and then chose that moment to divide time into B.C. and A.D.? What unique qualities existed that made this "the fulness of the time" [KJV]?

In his book *The Life and Teaching of Jesus Christ*, James Stewart suggests that there are several reasons to believe that Jesus could not have come at a better time in history.

First of all, it was the fullness of time politically. The Roman Empire had built great roads, spread the Greek language, and instilled its brand of *pax Romana* (Roman peace) wherever it went.

It was also the fullness of time morally. The world into which Jesus came, as graphically portrayed in Rom. 1, was morally void, wicked, and very much in need of a Savior.

Finally, it was the fullness of time religiously. The worship of Caesar had left a vacuum and created a hunger for spiritual things. The door was open, and the time was ripe.

Not a moment too early nor a moment too late. It was the Day of the Lord. No more waiting. Jesus had come at just the right time.

Some of you are waiting on the Lord right now. Maybe not 400 years, but you've been waiting a long time. You have been

praying prayers,

planning plans,

> hoping hopes,
> dreaming dreams,

but nothing has happened. So you wait. You don't really like it, but you don't know what else to do.

My word of hope for you today is that God always comes at just the right time. He may not come in your time, but He *will* come. That's a promise.

> Do you not know? Have you not heard? The Lord is the everlasting God, the Creator of the ends of the earth. He will not grow tired or weary, and his understanding no one can fathom. He gives strength to the weary and increases the power of the weak. Even youths grow tired and weary, and young men stumble and fall; but those who hope in [wait on] the Lord will renew their strength. They will soar on wings like eagles; they will run and not grow weary, they will walk and not be faint *(Isa. 40:28-31)*.

Jesus, You know how much we dislike waiting. We're not very patient. We want our prayers answered in two days or less! We dream big dreams, and we want to see them come true by next Thursday. At Christmas, help us remember that God always comes—even if it takes awhile.

O HOLY NIGHT

O holy night! the stars are brightly shining;
It is the night of the dear Savior's birth.
Long lay the world in sin and error pining,
Till He appeared and the soul felt its worth.

A thrill of hope—the weary world rejoices,
For yonder breaks a new and glorious morn!
Fall on your knees!
O hear the angel voices!
O night divine!
O night when Christ was born!
O night divine!
O night, O night divine!

The Wondrous Gift

Garage sale!

As soon as you hear those words, some of you start salivating, reach for your coats, and scream, "Let's go!" Others break out in a rash and run in the opposite direction, screaming, "Please! No!"

I fit nicely into that second category. I hate garage sales. Fortunately, I married someone who shares my total lack of interest in them. (One less thing to argue about.)

We have lots of friends, however, who love to get up early on Saturday morning and drive all over town looking for garage sales. At first glance, these people seem like good, normal, Christian people. But then you discover they have this chronic GSA problem: garage sale addiction.

I don't even like garage sales when they're at my house. I have to go out and try to staple a sign to a telephone pole that already has a gazillion staples in it. And I always seem to get the arrow pointing in the wrong direction.

Then there are the early morning sharks that seem to suddenly appear out of nowhere about 15 minutes before you're really ready. Boy, are they good! They drive a hard bargain and make you feel cheesy for asking a buck for something that cost you $40 just five years ago.

And then there's Cheryl trying to sell some of my favorite shirts—for 10 cents. What's she thinking? Some of those I actually wear once every 10 years. And those ties she sold 20 years ago—they're back in style now!

Obviously, one of the things I love most about Christmas is that it's usually too cold for garage sales. But let's back the truck up for a minute and take another look at this whole issue and try to find some redeemable quality about garage sales. As much as I dislike them (can you tell I'm trying to soften my attitude?), maybe we actually need them in order to get ready for Christmas. (This is painful, but I'm trying to keep an open mind.)

Is it possible that our lives are so full of stuff that we need to clear out our closets and throw out a bunch of junk in order to make room in our hearts for the wondrous gift of the newborn King and all the blessings He wants to give to us?

I read somewhere that Christian joy is not a matter of addition but subtraction. Most of the time when we're lacking joy we think we need to buy something new to make up for what's lacking: a new outfit, a new toy, a new car, a new piece of furniture. But the satisfaction is only temporary, because we always crave more.

We don't need more possessions—we need fewer desires. Instead of acquiring new stuff, we need to get rid of some old stuff, like—

old attitudes
old hurts
old temptations
old prejudices
old grudges
old addictions

Cleaning out some of that junk will really open up our hearts to some serious joy this Christmas. Having this kind of inward "garage sale" will create an empty, open, meek, hungry place inside us. And that's exactly the kind of place Christ longs to enter and fill. The question is—are we emptied-out enough to receive Him?

Jesus, I remember the time You met a guy who was too full of himself to need You. Essentially, You told him to go have a garage sale. But he hated garage sales. Forgive me for holding on to so much old stuff. I don't need to add—I need to subtract. I always want there to be room in my heart for You.

O LITTLE TOWN OF BETHLEHEM
How silently, how silently
The wondrous Gift is giv'n!
So God imparts to human hearts
The blessings of His heav'n.
No ear may hear His coming;
But in this world of sin,
Where meek souls will receive Him still,
The dear Christ enters in.

No Room

Wally was nine years old, a second grader. He was big and clumsy, slow in movement and mind. He was the kind of kid who, when the kids chose up sides to play ball, no one wanted.

Wally wanted badly to be in the church Christmas play. The director decided that since the innkeeper character didn't have many lines, maybe Wally could handle it.

On the night of the play an unusually large audience gathered for the Christmas production. Wally stood in the wings watching with fascination.

Then Joseph appeared, slowly, tenderly guiding Mary, and knocked hard on the wooden doors set into the backdrop.

"What do you want?" Wally the innkeeper said gruffly while swinging the door open.

"We seek lodging."

"Seek it elsewhere!" Wally looked straight ahead as he spoke. "The inn is full!"

"Sir, we've asked everywhere in vain. We have traveled far, and we are weary."

"There is no room in this inn for you," Wally said, properly stern.

"Please, good innkeeper—this is my wife, Mary. She is heavy with child. Surely you must have some corner for her to rest in."

Now for the first time, the innkeeper looked down at Mary. There was a pause long enough to make the audience tense with embarrassment.

"No! Be gone!" the prompter whispered from the wings.

"No!" Wally repeated. "Be gone!"

Joseph sadly placed his arm around Mary. Mary laid her head upon her husband's shoulder, and the two of them started to move away. Wally stood in the doorway, watching the forlorn couple. His mouth was open, his brow creased with concern, and his eyes filled unmistakably with tears. Suddenly this Christmas pageant became different from all the others.

"Don't go, Joseph!" Wally called out. "Bring Mary back!" He broke into a bright smile and exclaimed, "You can have my room!"

A few people thought the pageant had been ruined, but most folks thought it was the best pageant they had ever seen. You see, life becomes beautiful when we stop thinking only of ourselves and think of others ("No Room," *Guideposts*, December 1966, n.p. Reprinted with permission from *Guideposts*. Copyright © 1966 by Guideposts, Carmel, New York 10512. All rights reserved).

Someone has said that "joy" is spelled—

> **J**esus first
> **O**thers second
> **Y**ourself last

Precious Jesus, during this busy Christmas season, help me be more like Wally. Don't let me be a robot who just repeats the script from memory. Don't let me be so busy that I push for my way over Your ways or above the needs of others. Even in the crowds, help me see individuals who need a room or a smile or maybe a kind word!

THOU DIDST LEAVE THY THRONE
Thou didst leave Thy throne and
Thy kingly crown,
When Thou camest to earth for me;
But in Bethlehem's home there was found no room
For Thy holy nativity.
O come to my heart, Lord Jesus;
There is room in my heart for Thee.

For unto Us a Child Is Born

These next four devotionals fit together as a package and come from the beautiful chorus "For unto Us a Child Is Born" from Handel's *Messiah*. The words of this song come, of course, from Isa. 9:6: "For unto us a child is born, unto us a son is given: and the government shall be upon his shoulder: and his name shall be called Wonderful, Counsellor, The mighty God, The everlasting Father, The Prince of Peace" (KJV).

Each of these four pieces will explore a different facet of this scriptural and musical jewel. Rather than using Christmas carols, each devotional will close with a favorite hymn that highlights the focus of that piece.

Wonderful

What is it that really excites you? What is it that makes your heart race? When you get all happy inside, what is it that makes you feel that way? What is it that gets you so charged up that you can't stop talking about it?

For me, there's a long list of things that really light my fire: The New York Yankees, rhinos, walking on the beach, my family, Don Quixote, getting up early to see the first rays of the sun come over the horizon, a hazelnut latte, a good meal with close friends, praying with someone to accept Christ as Savior, and a Diet Coke from Sonic Drive-In.

How about you? What's on your list?

I'm sure that each of us could put together a list of favorite things. But during this Advent season I wish we could see Jesus as the One who excites us and thrills us more than anyone and anything else. It's so easy for us to allow other things to be the source of our excitement and joy. Not that they're wrong or bad. It's just that we may be getting our thrills from the wrong place.

I learned this lesson in a new way the time I got to meet Magic Johnson. A pastor friend of mine by the name of Phil Rogers had played on the same high school basketball team with Magic. One night Phil and I attended a Lakers game and were able to spend 20 minutes after the game talking with Magic outside the Lakers' locker room. Phil and Magic did most of the talking, and I just stood there like an idiot with my mouth open.

I was totally awestruck to be that close and that personal with one of the all-time NBA stars. I drove home the entire way, almost three hours, in total silence.

At first I was just speechless, flabbergasted, and blown away by the fact that I had just spent 20 minutes in the presence of one of the most well-known persons in the entire world at that time.

No sooner had I recognized this awe-inspired silence than I immediately became aware of an even more profound thought, one that brought tears of sadness flowing down my cheek.

Doug, why don't you feel that way about Jesus? Why isn't your heart filled with awe and wonder like that whenever you get to spend time in the presence of God Almighty? Magic's just a basketball player. How in the world does that compare with spending time with the Creator of the universe? And 20 minutes? When did God ever tell you He had to leave after granting you 20 minutes of His time?

My heart was broken. I felt ashamed for taking God so much for granted. Many times I get to be with Him in a deep intimate way. But seldom does that encounter produce the sense of awe it should.

I guess maybe I'm with Him too much to be speechless all the time. But ever since the night I spent

20 minutes with Magic Johnson, I try to be aware of what a privilege it is to spend time with God. Whether it's during my personal devotions or saying grace before a meal or kneeling at the altar for the pastoral prayer in a crowded sanctuary, I always try to remember that He's the one I want to thrill my life.

In the Christmas story, everyone who comes in contact with the Christ child is filled with awe and wonder: Mary, Joseph, the shepherds, Simeon, Anna, the magi. That's how I want it to be in my life.

Dearest Jesus, You are so wonderful. So amazing. So marvelous. So great. So awe-inspiring. So phenomenal. So much higher and greater than anyone or anything else in all my life. You're the One who always fills my life with unbelievable joy and hope. Please don't ever let me take You for granted. Again this Christmas, let my heart be overwhelmed and speechless. "For unto us a child is born, unto us a son is given: and the government shall be upon his shoulder. And his name shall be called Wonderful" (KJV).

ALL THAT THRILLS MY SOUL IS JESUS
Who can cheer the heart like Jesus,
By His presence all divine?
True and tender, pure and precious,
O how blest to call Him mine!
All that thrills my soul is Jesus;
He is more than life to me.
And the fairest of ten thousand
In my blessed Lord I see.

Counselor

Don't you love it when God has poured out so many blessings on your life that you feel as if you're going to burst with praise? These are times when you're on the mountaintop of your spiritual life.

Having grown up in West Virginia, I'm quite partial to mountains. I love the rugged terrain of my home state, especially in the fall when the trees look like a multicolored quilt covering the mountains in every direction.

I also enjoyed the privilege of having lived in the shadow of the Sierra Nevada Mountains of California for 20 years. Those snow-covered peaks with the rising sun glowing behind them is one my most memorable settings for early morning devotions.

As much as I love being on the mountaintop (especially Half Dome in Yosemite National Park), I've learned that life isn't always lived on the mountaintop. Sometimes new Christians experience life in such a new and wonderful way they think they can just stay on the mountaintop forever. But that's certainly not the case.

Valleys are also a significant part of the Christian life, times when all the joy of life seems to be residing in another zip code, all the bubbles have burst, and the clouds have hidden the sun.

You may feel as if the rug has been pulled out

from under you and you're just barely hanging on by your fingertips. "As for me, my feet had almost slipped; I had nearly lost my foothold" (Ps. 73:2).

It's right here that I love the fullness of the Christmas message. This Child who has been born, this Son that has been given is not only our "wonderful giver of joy" but is also the "Counselor" who comforts us in our time of deepest need.

When we've fallen off the mountain and almost lost our way, He's right beside us to catch us. "My flesh and my heart may fail, but God is the strength of my heart and my portion forever" (Ps. 73:26).

Although no one ever wishes for these difficult days in the valleys of life, it's actually these dark days of fear and suffering that draw us closer to God than ever before. When we discover that He is not only the God of the mountaintop but also Lord and Master over the valley, our love for Him will deepen in unbelievable ways.

When life breaks our hearts and leaves us for dead, we will learn just how much Jesus loves and cares for us. He will come to us in our time of need and be our Counselor and Healer.

Thank You, Jesus, for caring so much for us. Thank You for knowing where and when we need You the most. We certainly don't enjoy the valleys, but Your presence gives us the strength to keep going. Thank You for being a Light in the darkest nights. In Your name we pray. Amen!

DOES JESUS CARE?

Does Jesus care when my way is dark
With a nameless dread and fear?
As the daylight fades
Into deep night shades,
Does He care enough to be near?
O yes, He cares; I know He cares!
His heart is touched with my grief.
When they days are weary,
The long nights dreary,
I know my Savior cares.

Mighty God, Everlasting Father

From the very beginning of time, there has been a holy, loving God reaching out to create relationships with His people—walking in the garden with Adam and Eve, sailing with Noah, leading the way to the Promised Land with Abraham and the patriarchs, marching out of Egypt with Moses, going back home with Joshua, weeping with Jeremiah over the unfaithfulness of Israel, and being faithful to Daniel in the fiery furnace.

And then in the opening words of John's Gospel, we learn something even more fantastic: this God has taken the ultimate step in drawing close to us by becoming flesh and dwelling among us.

We're faced with the unexplainable fact that Jesus Christ is, as the theologians say, "very God and very Man." He is not half God and half man! He is Jesus Christ, the Son of God. But at the same time He is the mighty God, the everlasting Father. In himself He amazingly brings together all of humanity and all of divinity.

Paul takes his shot at trying to understand this mystery in Col. 1:15-17, 19: "He is the image of the invisible God, the firstborn over all creation. For by him all things were created. . . . He is before all things, and in him all things hold together. . . . For God was pleased to have all his fullness dwell in him."

My friend Millard Reed introduced me to an old poem titled "The Mystery of Incarnation," which highlights the paradox of Jesus, the God-Man.

He who is the Almighty
Became a suckling baby.
He who is all wise
Took on the dumbness of a newborn.
He whom the heavens cannot contain
Was enclosed in a woman's womb.
He before whom the seraphims continually cried holy,
*   holy, holy,*
Was born of a sinner into a world under the dominion of
*   sin.*
He who is unchanging went through nine months of con-
*   stant change*
To enter a world of change.
He who is all knowing had to communicate through baby
*   cries.*
He who is infinite became but a microscopic cell.
He who is love was born outside a hotel because no one had
*   room for His laboring mother.*
He who is the Creator became a creature.
He who has always been spirit took on the awkwardness of
*   a human body.*
He who is eternal allowed Himself to be bound by time.
He who is light was entombed for nine months in warm
*   blackness.*

He who is just was accused of being an illegitimate child.

He who is sovereign God became dependent upon a human man and woman for His food and clothing.

He who is clothed with majesty was born in a cattle trough.

He who alone is self-sufficient had to be cleaned and nursed.

He who is life was born with a death warrant around his neck.

Can there be a greater mystery?

Can there be a greater miracle?

Author unknown. Quoted in Millard Reed, *The Glory of His Presence* (Kansas City: Beacon Hill Press of Kansas City, n.d.), 29-30.

Jesus, You are amazing! You are the unique One who has brought divinity and humanity together. You are human enough to understand our battles and divine enough to win the battles! You and You alone have the credentials to be the right Man. We would not know how to live life without You!

A MIGHTY FORTRESS IS OUR GOD!
Did we in our own strength confide,
Our striving would be losing;
Were not the right Man on our side,
The Man of God's own choosing.
Dost ask who that may be?
Christ Jesus—it is He;
Lord Sabaoth, His name;
From age to age the same;
And He must win the battle.

Prince of Peace

The typical American family was trying to enjoy its very first trip to Disneyland—"the happiest place on earth." But today was the day that five-year-old Junior had decided to throw an all-out temper tantrum. (Something about Big Sister hitting him in the backseat on the drive from the hotel.)

As Mom pulled the crying kid down Disneyland's Main Street, she said to him, "You wanted to come here, and you're going to have fun whether you like it or not!"

I know a lot of people like that. They're supposed to be having fun, but most of the time they just feel like crying. Their lives are supposed to make sense, but sometimes the pieces don't seem to fit. They run their lives in ways that seem to make sense to them, but then they're surprised when they don't get the results they expected. It's like a poem titled *A Boy and His Stomach*, which my mom used to read to me when I was a little boy:

What's the matter, stummick?
Ain't I always been your friend?
Ain't I always been a partner to you?
All my pennies don't I spend
In getting nice things for you?
Don't I give you lots of cake?

Say, stummick, what's the matter,
You had to go an' ache?

Why, I loaded you with good things yesterday;
I gave you more corn an' chicken
Than you'd ever had before;
I gave you fruit and candy,
Apple pie an' chocolate cake,
An' last night when I got to bed
You had to go an' ache.

Say, what's the matter with you?
Ain't you satisfied at all?
I gave you all you wanted;
You was hard jes' like a ball,
An' you couldn't hold another bit of puddin'
Yet last night
You ached most awful, stummick!
That ain't treatin' me jest right.

I've been a friend to you, I have!
Why ain't you a friend o' mine?
They gave me castor oil becoz you made me whine.
I'm feelin' fine this mornin';
Yes, it's true;
But I tell you, stummick, you better appreciate
The things I do for you.

—Edgar A. Guest

From *Poems Teachers Ask For: Book 1* (Danville, N.Y.: F. A. Owen Publishing Co., n.d.), 93.

We sometimes pay a high price to buy the best that life has to offer, but then we can't understand why life turns around and spits in our faces. Examples are all around us:

- The father who's too wrapped up in his job to spend time just listening to his daughter may discover too late that he wasted his chances to enjoy one of life's most gratifying experiences.

- The mom who is so busy keeping her house in order that she never allows her boys to wrestle and roughhouse may one day realize she missed out on a lot of laughter.

- The couple who decides to get ahead even if it means working so many hours that they don't have the quality of time for deep intimacy may discover that while they were keeping up with the Joneses, their marriage was going down the tubes.

- Teenagers who use their freedom to cultivate unhealthy friendships and live outside parental boundaries may wake up to find that their destructive practices have created life patterns that are hard to break.

When our broken, confused lives are filled with more chaos than character, Jesus wants to come to us as the Prince of Peace. When it seems like all the pieces are scrambled and scattered, He offers a peace that brings restoration and harmony.

This Jesus, whose birth we celebrate this Christmas season, is the One (the only one) who can straighten out all that is crooked in our lives. It is in His will and His life that we will find the peace we're looking for. It is this peace that brings the fun back to life, whether or not we get to spend the day at Disneyland.

Jesus, thank You for bringing peace to all of the storms of life. Without You as the center point of my life, I would run crazily in all directions. Your peace brings order to my chaos and fulfillment to the empty places. Help me with the storms that may be brewing on the horizon. In Your name I pray. Amen.

WONDERFUL PEACE
Ah! soul, are you here without comfort or rest,
    Marching down the rough pathway of time?
Make Jesus your Friend ere the shadows grow dark.
    O accept this sweet peace so sublime!
        Peace! peace! wonderful peace,
    Coming down from the Father above!
Sweep over my spirit forever, I pray,
    In fathomless billows of love.

God Is Not Dead!

The first day I started working on this Christmas devotional book, I took my hymnal and my Bible to one of my favorite coffee shops to look through the Christmas carols to seek inspiration for the writing assignment that lay ahead of me.

As I turned the pages, it became apparent that in every carol was a hosanna moment that stood out above all the rest. Each carol had its own crescendo point. Sometimes it was obvious; other times it was hidden away in the third verse. As I sipped my latte, I felt the passion of such phrases as

- *O come to my heart, Lord Jesus;*
  There is room in my heart for Thee.
- *Be near me, Lord Jesus.*
- *He comes to make His blessings flow*
  Far as the curse is found.
- *The hopes and fears of all the years*
- *Disperse the gloomy clouds of night,*
  And death's dark shadows put to flight.
- *A thrill of hope*
- *For the manger of Bethlehem cradles a King!*
- *Veiled in flesh the Godhead see*
- *O rest beside the weary road*
  And hear the angels sing.

It was a moving experience to discover the one

phrase in each carol that seemed to tower over all the rest of the song.

But there was one carol that would not yield its pearl to my probing. I read it over and over, asking the question "Where is the crescendo?"

With every reading, the tears flowed until I realized two things: first, there's no way to isolate or highlight only one phrase or verse of this song. It has to be kept together as a whole piece, telling one story. And second, this song has become my favorite Christmas carol.

The carol I have saved for last is *I Heard the Bells on Christmas Day*. The words were written by distinguished American poet Henry Wadsworth Longfellow on Christmas Day 1864 in the depths of the Civil War. Not only was the nation troubled by the despair of war, but Longfellow was personally heartbroken over the tragic death of his wife, Francis, and the crippling war injury of his son, Charles.

His poem was originally titled "Christmas Bells" and contained two additional stanzas, which were later omitted because of their specific references to the Civil War. The poem was set to music in 1872 by John B. Calkin to give us the carol we enjoy today.

Whatever the age, men and women of all nations and races want to experience "peace on earth, good will to men." However, there are times of war and great tragedy that often cause us to almost lose all hope.

Even though Longfellow obviously knew what it was like to feel the depths of despair, he still would not let go of his faith in God. Even in the darkest night, even when circumstances would want to laugh at us and mock us for holding onto our faith, Longfellow says that not only is God not dead, but He's not even asleep. Even when this God seems silent or far away, He can still be trusted.

We have read the end of the Book. We know who wins. We know that "the wrong shall fail, the right prevail." This Christ for whom the bells ring out on this Christmas Day will come forth as the Victor over sin, death, hell, and the grave.

The Christ who came down on Christmas is the Christ who rose up on Easter Sunday. And one day the bells will sound His coming again!

Whatever difficult or tragic situation you and I face this Christmas season, the victorious Christ wants to say to us, *Hear My voice, hear My chime, and hear My chant! I will bring peace on earth. I will bring good will to people everywhere.*

Victory in Jesus, my Savior forever! Thank You for the eternal hope that You give us. In the midst of our despair and hopelessness, You bring peace. If you're not dead, then hope is not dead! The "Christmas Bells" will remind me again this year that I can trust in You! Thank You for inspiring Henry Wadsworth Longfellow with these beautiful words.

I HEARD THE BELLS
ON CHRISTMAS DAY

I heard the bells on Christmas day
Their old familiar carols play,
And wild and sweet the words repeat
Of peace on earth, goodwill to men.

I tho't how, as the day had come,
The belfries of all Christendom
Had rolled along th'unbroken song
Of peace on earth, goodwill to men.

And in despair I bowed my head.
"There is no peace on earth," I said,
"For hate is strong, and mocks the song
Of peace on earth, goodwill to men."

Then pealed the bells more loud and deep:
"God is not dead, nor doth He sleep;
The wrong shall fail, the right prevail,
With peace on earth, goodwill to men."

Till. ringing, singing on its way,
The world revolved from night to day—
A voice, a chime, a chant sublime,
Of peace on earth, goodwill to men!

Advent Liturgies

The four Sundays of Advent offer us the opportunity to prepare our hearts for the coming of the Christ child.

In the following pages you have five Advent liturgies, one for each Sunday of Advent as well as one for Christmas Eve. Each reading focuses on a key word that guides your celebration for that day.

First Sunday of Advent: Anticipation
Second Sunday of Advent: Open
Third Sunday of Advent: Surprise
Fourth Sunday of Advent: Emmanuel
Christmas Eve: Light

You are encouraged to use these readings in your family devotions throughout the Christmas season. If your church does not celebrate Advent with readings like this, you might want to incorporate these into your worship services. The liturgies can be read by family members or a couple of teenagers.

You might even want to try your hand at writing your own liturgical readings. That is a wonderful avenue to express the emotions surrounding the coming of the Messiah.

Advent Candle Liturgy
First Sunday of Advent

First Reader:

We have gathered on this first Sunday to celebrate the coming of joy into our world.

Second Reader:

The key word for this first Sunday is *anticipation*. For thousands of years, people waited in anticipation for the Messiah to come. And so it is that we, too, anticipate His coming.

First Reader:

To some, these days may be nothing more than a "countdown to Christmas," an agony to endure until the real celebration begins. But the Advent season serves to remind us that the Christ who came to redeem us will come again to receive us to himself.

Second Reader:

As you anticipate the coming Christmas, remember our Savior's Advent promise: "I go to prepare a place for you" (John 14:2, KJV).

First Reader:

Just as God's people long ago awaited the Messiah's first coming, so we today await His second coming. We, too, live in anticipation.

Second Reader:

> O come, O come, Emmanuel,
> And ransom captive Israel,
> That mourns in lonely exile here
> Until the Son of God appear.
> Rejoice! Rejoice! Emmanuel
> Shall come to thee, O Israel!

Advent Candle Liturgy
Second Sunday of Advent

First Reader:

We welcome you on this second Sunday of Advent. The key word for this Sunday is *open*.

Second Reader:

Christmas is a time of "opening." We open our presents, we open doors to all our company, and we open our hearts.

First Reader:

Opening our hearts may be the most difficult of all. Even at Christmas it's possible to become selfish and self-centered, more concerned about getting than giving.

Second Reader:

We may need to be reminded that everything we celebrate was made possible because "God so loved the world, that he gave" (John 3:16, KJV).

First Reader:

He opened His heart in concern for all humanity. He opened the womb of a virgin to deliver His Son to our world.

Second Reader:

This Son, Jesus, opened His arms to love and then to be nailed to a cross until God opened the tomb to bring Him out alive.

First Reader:

Heaven itself is open to us now, where our Savior waits with open arms to receive us to himself. Will you open your heart this Christmas to God's love for you?

Second Reader:

> *Silently now I wait for Thee*
> *Ready, my God, Thy will to see.*
> *Open my eyes; illumine me,*
> *Spirit divine.*

—Clara H. Scott

Advent Candle Liturgy
Third Sunday of Advent

First Reader:

Today we celebrate the third Sunday of Advent. The key word for this Sunday is *surprise.*

Second Reader:

Our God has a reputation for doing the unexpected. Mary was certainly surprised when the angel informed her that she was going to have a baby.

First Reader:

Our Lord's life on earth was full of surprises: sick people were healed, hungry people were comforted, and even dead people were raised to life again.

Second Reader:

Soon you will be opening Christmas gifts. Some of them will be a surprise, others perhaps not because you hinted or maybe even peeked.

First Reader:

Even though we already know how much God loves us, the best is still ahead. He still has new things planned. No matter how much we look forward to it, God will certainly surprise us by making heaven far greater than we ever dreamed.

Second Reader:

> *While shepherds watched their flocks by night,*
> *   All seated on the ground,*
> *The angel of the Lord came down,*
> *   And glory shone around.*
> *"Fear not," said he, for mighty dread*
> *   Had seized their troubled mind,*
> *"Glad tidings of great joy I bring*
> *   To you and all mankind."*

—Nahum Tate

Advent Candle Liturgy
Fourth Sunday of Advent

First Reader:

We welcome you on this fourth Sunday of Advent. Today's word is *Emmanuel*.

93

Second Reader:

Emmanuel means "God is with us." The angels announced it over Bethlehem, and at the manger the shepherds saw that it was true. They were only the first of many.

First Reader:

The hungry, the sick, the troubled, the confused, the hopeless, the discouraged, the broken, the lost, and the lonely: Jesus came to bring God to all these.

Second Reader:

Even in the pushing and shoving crowds in the mall, even in the crowded rows of the sanctuary this morning, there can be individuals who are very broken, lost, and lonely.

First Reader:

If you're far away from home, if you're a single parent, if you're facing your first Christmas without a loved one, if you're feeling lonely for any reason, remember *Emmanuel* this Christmas. God *is* with you!

Second Reader:

> *O holy Child of Bethlehem,*
> *Descend on us, we pray.*
> *Cast out our sin, and enter in;*
> *Be born in us today.*
> *We hear the Christmas angels*
> *The great glad tidings tell.*
> *O come to us; abide with us,*
> *Our Lord, Emmanuel.*
> —Phillips Brooks

Advent Candle Liturgy
Christmas Eve

First Reader:

We welcome you to this Christmas Eve worship service as we celebrate the birth of our Savior. Our key word for tonight is *light.*

Second Reader:

Have you noticed how bright the Christmas season is? Even though darkness comes earlier each night as the days shorten into winter, the lights of Christmas push back the darkness with their special glow.

First Reader:

And have you noticed that it doesn't take large glaring spotlights to make the season so bright? A lot of little lights will accomplish the same purpose, each adding its own small luster to the total brilliance.

Second Reader:

In the same way, the light of Christ's presence in the manger was not spectacular. He was just "the little Lord Jesus asleep on the hay."

First Reader:

And yet the life He lived for us and the life He gave to us are as bright as heaven itself.

Second Reader:

And so He calls each of us to let our light shine. It may be small, but as each of us adds our glow to that of others, the light can be large.

First Reader:

> One small child in a land of a thousand
> One small dream of a Savior tonight
> One small hand reaching out to the starlight
> One small city of life.

Second Reader:

> One small light from the flame of a candle
> One small light from a city of might
> One small light from the stars in the endless night
> One small light from a face.*
>
> —David Meece